10 Guidelines On How to Receive From God

10 Guidelines On How to Receive From God

LARRY ELLERBEE

Copyright © 2011 by Larry Ellerbee.

Library of Congress Control Number:		2011902920
ISBN:	Hardcover	978-1-4568-7470-4
	Softcover	978-1-4568-7469-8
	Ebook	978-1-4568-7471-1

All rights reserved. No part of this book may be reproduced or transmitted in any form or by any means, electronic or mechanical, including photocopying, recording, or by any information storage and retrieval system, without permission in writing from the copyright owner.

This book was printed in the United States of America.

To order additional copies of this book, contact:
Xlibris Corporation
1-888-795-4274
www.Xlibris.com
Orders@Xlibris.com
94319

CONTENTS

1. Love .... Faith worked by love 9

2. Believe .... Children of God 14

3. Live Holy .... Living in sin, out of His will 18

4. Obedience .... Obey the Word of God 21

5. Trust .... Blessed is the man that trust in the Lord 24

6. Faith .... Without faith, it is impossible to please God 28

7. Patience .... If you don't have patience, you'll give up 32

8. Be A Giver .... God blesses a cheerful giver 35

9. Ask 39

10. Thanksgiving and Praise 43

Introduction

Receiving Isn't Automatic

THERE ARE SOME things you must do in order to receive from God. Receiving from God is easy. Receiving God's best is up to you. You can start receiving from God, today. If you will follow the Guidelines in this book, God will bless you in every area of your life. These Guidelines worked for me and they will work for you. When you follow these Guidelines, God will answer your prayers. God promised that he will take care of you, heal you, save you, and supply all of your needs. Whatever you need from God is available every minute, every hour, and every day. The Word of God can set you free from sickness, disease, poverty or lack, fear, and depression. The Word of God can deliver you from sin, sickness, death, drugs, alcohol, and cigarettes. The Word of God can change your life, financially, spiritually, socially, and mentally. The 'Word of God is powerful. I have written these Guidelines based on the Word of God. You must study the Word of God for yourself to find out what God's purpose and plan is for your life. Jesus said, "If you continue in my word, you shall know the truth and the truth shall set you free." John 8:31, 32. God is a giver, God gives good gifts to his children, but there are many who aren't receiving his blessings. You pray, but there is no answer, you have fasted, and there are no results. You may be wondering why you haven't received. You may be blaming God because your prayers go unanswered. Whatever the reason may be, DON'T BLAME GOD. God is not your problem. God is the answer to your problems. God never makes mistakes; God loves you and wants you to have the best in life. That's why Jesus came that we might have life and have it more abundantly (John 10:10). Now is the time to take control over your life. If you follow these Guidelines, you will receive the desires of your heart.

One

Love

<u>Galatians 5:6 Faith worked by love</u>

D O YOU KNOW why your faith isn't working? You have been **praying** and **praying**, but you're not getting any answers. You **fast** and **pray**, but no answers. You **praise** the lord, but there are no blessing coming down. If you have **<u>unforgiveness</u>** in your heart, then your faith will not work for you. You must love everyone, even your enemies. Jesus said, "**<u>Love</u>** your enemies, bless them that curse you, do good to them that hate you, and pray for them which despitefully use you, and persecute you." Matthew 5:44

We know that you must have **<u>faith</u>** to receive from God. To get your faith to work for you, **<u>you must walk in love</u>**.

<u>Love is Powerful</u>

God loves you, He cares about you, and God wants you to have the best in life. God doesn't want His people to struggle in life. God wants His children to prosper and be in good health. (III John 3:2). God knows that your faith will not work for you if you're not walking in love. If you aren't walking in love, then you're not walking in faith. Faith pleases God. You have faith; God hath dealt to everyman the measure of faith. (Roman 12:3). But, everyone doesn't walk in love.

God is love

God revealed His love towards us when He sent His only begotten son, Jesus, into the world, that we might live through him. This is love, not that we love God, but that He loves us. If God loves us, we ought to love one another. If we love one another, God lives in us by the spirit he has given us. (I John 4: 9-13)

You have the Love of God in your heart. (Roman 5:5)

Jesus said if you love me, you will keep my commandments. (John 14:15)

If you walk in the Love of God, you will obey His Word and God will bless you.

Love is the Key to Receiving

Whatsoever we ask, we receive of Him because we keep or obey his commandments, and do those things that are pleasing in His sight and this is the commandment that we should believe on the name of His son, Jesus Christ and love one another as he gave us commandments. (I John 3:24)

When you're walking in the Love of God, you will do those things that are pleasing in his sight, you can go before God and ask anything and He will give it to you. What do you need today? A financial blessing, healing, joy, peace, a love one saved? Deliverance from drugs, cigarettes, sin, fear? God said whatsoever we ask, we **receive** from him. Whatever God says in His Word, do it.

Love is the Greatest Gift
I Corinthians 13: 1-13

This whole chapter talks about charity. Charity means **love**. Let's look at a few of these verses in this scripture.

Verse 1—Though I speak with the tongues of men and of angels and have not charity (**love**)

I have become a sounding brass or tinking cymbal.

Though I have the gift of speech, I can motivate people, I can encourage people. The words I speak may sound good, it may even change your life, but if I don't have charity (**love**), I am not doing nothing but making noise.

Verse 2—Though I have the **Gift of Prophecy**, and understand all mysteries, and all **Knowledge**, and though I have **all faith**. So I could remove mountains and have not charity (**love**), I am nothing.

Though I have the **Gift of Prophecy**, I can prophesy and tell you the will of God for your life. I can tell you what's going to happen in the future, but if I have not charity (**love**), I am nothing.

Though I have the **Gift of Knowledge**, I know the Word of God. I know some things that you don't know. Some people call me "Know-It-All", but if I have not charity (**love**), I am nothing.

Thought I have **all faith**, I can speak the Word of God over any problem or circumstance and it shall obey me. I have faith for healing, prosperity, and salvation. I have **all faith**, but if I have not charity (**love**), I am nothing.

Verse 3—And though I bestow all of my goods **to feed the poor** and have not charity (**love**) it **profited me nothing**.

It doesn't matter how much money you give to the poor, you can give your last dime or you can give millions, you can feed the poor, and you can even buy clothes for the poor, but if you have not charity (**love**), it profits you nothing.

Verse 7—**Believeth all things**

I know some of you don't believe the things that I am saying, because you are not walking in **love**. If you are walking in **love**, you'll believe everything **God said** in His Word. You believe God can save, you believe God can heal the sick, you believe God can raise the dead.

Do you believe God when it comes to giving and receiving?

Do you believe that God can bless you financially?

Love Believeth All Things

Verse 8—**Love never faileth**

If you are walking in the Love of God, you will never fail. Imagine never failing. Everything you put your hands to, prospers. You can accomplish all your goals in this life.

Verse 13—And now abideth faith, hope, charity (**love**) these three: but the greatest of those is charity (**love**)

The Command to Love

These things I command you, that ye love one another. (John 15:17)

Remember This

If a man says, I love God, and hateth his brother, he is a liar: For he that loveth not his brother whom he hath seen; how can he love God whom he hath not seen? And this commandment we have from him, that he who loveth God loves his brother also. I John 4: 20, 21

Two

Believe

<u>Born Again Believer</u>

B ECAUSE JESUS SAID, "He that is not with me is against me," God is going to use his children to get the Gospel spread unto all nations. It is going to take a lot of money. God is looking for those He can trust with His money, those who have been faithful in their giving.

<u>"The wealth of the sinner is laid up for you."</u>
<u>Proverbs 13:22</u>

I know you think that the sinners own everything, but they do not. I know they have the big houses, the best cars, the big businesses, the best jobs, the land, and the big bank accounts. Don't get mad because the sinners prosper, all of that is going to change, leave them alone, let them store it up, you know who they are storing it up for (**<u>the just</u>**). In these last days, God is going to take it from them and give it to his children.

<u>"God is going to turn the tables." Psalm 23:5</u>

God prepared the table for us in the presence of our enemies. When God takes it from them, they are going to be mad and broke. Who are they going to be mad with? **<u>YOU</u>**! The reason I say this, is because of the hundredfold return.

<u>The Hundredfold Return</u>
<u>(Matthew 19:29, Matthew 13:8, 23)</u>

Jesus said we shall receive a hundredfold, **now is the time.** "Houses and brethren, and sisters and mothers, and children, and lands with persecutions; and in the world to come with eternal life." (Mark 10:29, 30) I know Jesus said houses and land with persecutions. I am going to add this list . . . the best cars, the big businesses, the best jobs, the big bank accounts for his children. When God blesses you with the hundredfold return, you're able to help get the Gospel spread into all nations.

God owns EVERYTHING

"The Earth is the Lord and the fullness there of. The world and they that dwell therein." Psalm 24:1

The sinners don't own anything. God owns the whole world and everything in it, including you. God created all the wealth of this earth, He didn't create it for the unbelievers who are hard hearted sinful people who deny Him and disobey His Word. God wants His children to prosper; God doesn't want His children to do without. God is no different from any other father. He wants His children to have the best.

God created everything for His children

In the beginning, when God created this world, He created it for Adam. **Adam had everything that he needed** in the Garden of Eden. God told Adam that he can eat off any tree in the Garden, but the Tree of Good and Evil, do not eat of this tree, but the Devil came to Adam and his wife and lied to them. The Devil told them that if they ate of the Tree of Good and Evil, they would be like God and they wouldn't die. They believed the lie of the Devil and ate of the Tree of Good and Evil. When Adam sinned and disobeyed God, God put him out of the Garden and made him go to work. When Adam sinned and disobeyed God, he lost his authority. He turned that authority over to the devil. (Genesis 3)

The Purpose

"For this purpose God sent Jesus into the world, that He might destroy the works of the Devil." (I John 3:8-10) The thief (which is the devil) cometh not, but **to steal** and **to kill** and **destroy**: "I (**Jesus**) am come that they might have **life** and have it **more abundantly**." (John 10:10)

God sent Jesus into the world to take back what the Devil had stolen from Adam. Jesus came that we may have eternal life and live more abundantly, a life of blessing, **no lack**, everything you need in abundance.

God's covenant with Abraham still valid

The New Testament teaches that Jesus paid the price for us. All Christians are heirs to the same blessing that Abraham received from God. That the blessing of Abraham might come on the Gentiles through Jesus Christ. (Galatians 3:14)

"And if ye be Christ's, then are ye Abraham's seed, and heirs according to the promise." Galatians 3:29

We inherit God's blessing

God's Word clearly tells us that we are heirs to Abraham. This means that the blessings God gave to Abraham are available to us. Our father wants us to receive the same blessing that he gave Abraham and we can receive these blessings if we follow His Guidelines.

You must be born into God's spiritual family

You must be born of the spirit of God to receive his blessing. You must repent of your sins and ask God to forgive you for all sins known and unknown. If you confess with your mouth, the Lord Jesus, and believe in your heart, that God raised Jesus from the dead, you shall be saved.

For with the heart man believeth unto righteousness; and with the mouth confession is made unto salvation. (Roman 10:9, 10)

When you become a child of God, then you can go to your father and ask Him to bless you in every area of your life. If you follow these Guidelines, God will hear and answer your prayers.

Three

Live Holy

THERE IS NO one as holy as the Lord, for there is none besides thee; neither is there any rock like our God. (I Samuel 2:2) Who is like unto thee, o Lord among the Gods? Who is like thee, **glorious in holiness**, fearful in praises, doing wonders. (Exodus 15:11)

There is no one as holy as the Lord, there are no other God's who can come close to his holiness. **God is holy** and God wants His children to be holy, live holy, walk holy, talk holy, and act holy. God wants His children to be just like him. God said, in Leviticus 20:7, "Sanctify yourselves therefore, and be ye holy: For I am the Lord your God." If God says to be holy, then you can be holy. Stop saying you can't live a holy life. You can live a holy life and God knows you can. You can start by taking one day at a time. Do not worry, if you sin, just confess it and God will forgive you. You will learn from your mistakes as you continue to grow in the Lord.

To live a holy life, you must separate yourself from sin. God hates sin. **God will not bless you, if you are living a sinful lifestyle**.

Sin—means—thoughts or behaviors which are contrary to the glory or character of God; To commit to an offense against God's law.

Holy—means—uniquely divine; **separated from sin**: morally perfect; consecrated to God

"For all have sinned and come short of the Glory of God." (Roman 3:23). If we say that we have no sin, we deceive ourselves, and the truth in not in us. If we confess our sins, He is faithful and just to forgive us our sins, and to cleanse us from all unrighteousness. (I John 1:8, 9)

When we sin, we must confess our sins to the Father and He will forgive us. If you don't confess your sins, God will not forgive you and God will not hear your prayers. If I regard iniquity (**sin**) in my heart, the Lord will not hear me. (Psalm 66:18)

If God doesn't hear your prayer, then how is He going to bless you? Sin will hinder your prayers.

Be holy and without blame

According as he hath chosen us in Him before the foundation of the world, that we should **be holy and without blame** before him **in love**. Ephesians 1:4

Who hath **saved us** and **called us** with a holy calling, not according to our works, but according **to his own purpose** and grace, which was given to us in Christ Jesus before the world began.

Even before God created the world, He wanted his children to be holy and without blame. He sent Jesus to save us from the penalty of sin, which is death. God called us with **a holy calling** for his own purpose.

Consecrated—means—dedication to God's service

Know ye not that ye are the Temple of God and the Spirit of God dwelleth in you? If any man defile the Temple of God, him shall God destroy: For the Temple of God is holy, which temple ye are. (I Corinthians 3:16, 17). Your body is the Temple of God, the Holy Spirit lives inside of you. The Temple which is your body is holy. I didn't say it, God said it.

A living sacrifice

You must present your body to God as a living sacrifice holy, acceptable to God which is your reasonable service. Your body is the Temple of God, God's spirit lives in you, you must honor God by taking care of your body. You must not defile your body by eating or drinking anything that causes harm to your body. If you walk in the spirit, you will not fulfill the lust of the flesh, because greater is He that is in you, than He that's in the world.

The Holy Spirit in you is greater than sin, sickness, and disease.
The Holy Spirit in you is greater than any circumstance you might face.
The Holy Spirit in you is greater than anything this life can throw at you.
The Holy Spirit in you is the same Holy Spirit that created the World.
The Holy Spirit in you can help you accomplish all your goals in life.
The Holy Spirit is your helper.

If you are a child of God,
If you are living a holy life,
If you are a faithful giver,
If you follow these Guidelines in this book,
I believe you can go before God and ask Him for anything according to His will. He will give it to you.

Four

Obedience

"If they obey and serve him, they shall spend their days in prosperity and their years in pleasures." (Job 36:11)

IF YOU WILL listen to God and obey him, you will be blessed with prosperity throughout your life.

We fail to receive God blessing simply because we don't step out in faith and do what His Word says to do.

If we really believe God, then we'll do what God's Word tells us to do.

The bible is our Instruction Book. If you follow the instructions that are outlined in this book, you will receive the blessings of the lord.

All these blessings will come upon you and overtake you if you will listen and obey God's commands, you will be blessed coming in, blessed going out, the Lord will make you the head and not the tail, above and not beneath and you shall be the lender and not the borrower. (Deuteronomy 28:1-15)

"If you be willing and obedient, ye shall eat the good of the land." (Isaiah 1:19)

Are you willing to obey God's Word? If you obey God's Word you can eat the good of the land, you can have the best this world has to offer.

Strong faith demands action

"Be ye doers of the Word, and not hearers only, deceiving your own selves." (James 1:22)

If we just listen to God's Word and don't do what it says to do, we deceive ourselves.

Do not deceive yourselves by just listening to the Word. Instead, put it into practice. Whosoever listens to the Word, but does not put it into practice is like a man who looks in the mirror and sees himself as he is, he takes a good look at himself and then goes away and at once forgets what he looks like. But whosoever looks loosely into the perfect law that set people free, who keeps on paying attention to it and does not simply listen and then forget it, but puts it into practice, that person will be **blessed by God in what he does**. (**GNB**)

We must be like Jesus

Jesus said, "I do nothing of myself: but as my father (**God**) hath taught me, I speak these things. He that sent me is with me; the Father hath not left me alone; For I always do those things that please him." (John 8:28, 29) How did Jesus please the Father?

Jesus obeyed God, Jesus said, "The father hath taught me, I only speak what he tells me to speak, Jesus said I do nothing of myself. The father dwelleth in me, He doeth the works." (John 14:10)

We ought to obey God rather than men

Jesus told the disciples to go into the entire world and preach the Gospel to everyone. Jesus said, "These signs shall follow them that believe; In my name they shall cast out devils: They shall lay hands on the sick and they shall recover." (Mark 16:15-20)

And it came to pass that the high priest, the rulers and elders were grieved that they taught the people and preached the name of Jesus. They laid hands on them and put them in jail. Peter and John had to go before the council, the high priest, the rulers, and the elders asked the disciples, **by what power** or **by what name** did you heal the impotent man. Peter told the high priest and the elders of Israel **by the name of Jesus** this man is made whole. The high priest threaten them, and commanded them not to speak nor teach in the name of Jesus, but Peter and John answered and said unto them **it's not right in the sight of God to listen unto you more than unto God**. For we cannot, but speak the things which we have **seen** and **heard**. The high priest threatened them further, then they let them go. But the disciples **continue to speak the word with boldness**, healing the sick, casting out unclean spirits (**devils**) in the name of Jesus. By the hands of Peter and John were many signs and wonders wrought among the people. When the high priest heard that they continued to speak in the name of Jesus. They laid hold of them and put them in prison again, but **the angel of the Lord** let them out of prison. They found and arrested them again and when they had brought them before the council: The high priest asked them saying, "Didn't we tell you not speak or teach in the name of Jesus," then Peter and the Apostles answered and said, "We ought to **obey God rather than men**." The disciples obeyed Jesus' command. They did everything that Jesus told them to do.

Receive your rewards

"Whatsoever ye do, do it heartily, as to the Lord, and not unto men, knowing that of the Lord ye shall receive the reward of the inheritance for Ye serve The Lord Christ." (Colossians 3:23, 24)

Five

Trust

"Blessed is the man that trusteth in the Lord" (Jeremiah 17:7)

WHEN YOU PUT your trust in the Lord, you are blessed, you are happy, there is no lack in your life, all your needs are met, you are living the good life.

The Lord wants you to trust him for everything. If you need **healing**—trust the Lord to heal you. If you need **money**—trust the Lord to give you that money. If you need **your loved ones saved**—trust the Lord to save them. If you need **boldness**—to witness, to speak His Word, to do His perfect will—trust the Lord to give you boldness. If you need the Lord **to deliver** you from bad habits or sin—trust the Lord to deliver you.

Let me give you an "example"
On how you trust God's Word and
how to stand on God's Word

Let's take the word **salvation**. When you Got saved, you confessed:

Roman 10:9—If you shall confess with thy mouth the Lord Jesus, and shall believe in thine heart that God hath raised Him from the dead, thou shall be saved.

Some of you have been standing on that one scripture for 5, 10, 20, 30, 50 years. Nobody can take that **word** from you. People have talked about you like a dog. They have called you names, but you are still standing on that **word Roman 10:9**. Nothing can move you off that word. It rooted and grounded in your heart. When it comes to your healing, money, loves one's saved, deliverance, or whatever it is, you have to believe the Word of God the same way you believe God for salvation.

Go find scriptures that pertain to what you need in life. Like, healing, money, salvation, food, or clothes.

You must trust the Word of God and stand on it, and God will give you the desires of your heart.

"Trust the Lord at all times" (Psalm 62:8)

Sometimes we go through trials and hard times, no matter what the situation may look like or what the circumstance or problems may be, we must continue to trust in the Lord at all times. Jesus said, "Therefore take no thought, saying, What shall we eat? Or, What shall we drink? Or, Wherewithal shall we be clothed? (For after all these things do the gentiles seek:) for your heavenly Father knoweth that we have need of all these things, but seek ye first the kingdom of God, and his righteousness, and all these things shall be added unto you." (Matthew 6:31-33). When you put your trust in God and seek first the kingdom of God, everything that you need in life will be granted unto you because you turn to him first for help.

Trust—means—to put one's confidence in

And this is the confidence that we have in Him, that if we ask anything according to His will, he hearth us: and if we know that he hear us: whatsoever we ask, we know that we have the petition that we desired of him.

Who do you put your confidence in or who do you put your trust in?

Some people put their trust in different things like their job, money, social security check, the welfare system, their business and retirement check. If you put your trust in these things, you will fail to receive what God has in store for you. God wants you to put your trust completely in him, because you can lose your job, then your money will be cut off, the government can stop your social security check, stop welfare, your business could fail, your retirement could stop, then you will struggle though life because you put your trust in these material things.

Some people put their trust in: man, family, friends, co-workers, and their spouse. Don't listen to unbelievers who don't know God, who don't know anything about trusting God. If you go to them for advice and what they are saying doesn't line up with the Word of God, don't listen to them. Sometimes you can't listen to believers (Christians) who don't trust God, who don't trust the Word of God. There are some who can change the truth of God's Word into a lie. God also wants you to stop listening to the lies of the devil because the devil hates the truth, there is no truth in him, and he is the father of liars. Listen to those who believe the Word of God, who trust God and obey him.

Trust God, not man

"God is not a man, that he should lie, neither the son of man that he should repent: Hath he said and shall he not do it? Or hath he spoken, and shall he not make it good?" (Numbers 23:19) God doesn't change His mind like humans do, has he ever promised, without doing what he said. "**It is better to trust in the Lord, than to put confidence in man**." (Psalm 118:8)

In God we trust

Look at the dollar bill—it says "**In God we trust**." To some it says—"**In money we trust**." Some people trust in the mighty dollar, instead of trusting in the mighty God. Instead of thinking what can the mighty dollar do for me, you should be thinking what can the mighty God do to supply all your needs, **The Mighty God**—has no limits, God is your source, God supplies all needs and all things are possible to him that believeth.

"Trust in the Lord with all your heart and lean not unto your own understanding. In all thy ways acknowledge Him, and he shall direct thy paths." (Proverb 3: 5,6)

Amplified Bible

Lean on, trust in, and be confident in the Lord with all your heart and mind and do not rely on your own insight and understanding, in all your ways, recognize and acknowledge him and he will direct and make straight and plan your paths.

"O taste and see that the Lord is Good: Blessed is the man that trusteth in Him." (Psalm 34:8) When you trust in the Lord, you will begin to taste and see the goodness of the Lord.

Six

Faith

" . . . God hath dealt to every man the measure of faith." (Roman 12:3)

IF YOU ARE born again, you have faith, you might not be using your faith, but you do have it.

Jesus—dealt with people who had **small faith**. Some had **little faith** and some who had **great faith**.

Everything that we receive from God is by faith

Now faith is the substance of things hoped for, the evidence of things not seen. (Hebrew 11:7)

We receive **salvation** by faith, **money** by faith, **healing** by faith, **answers to your prayers** by faith.

When you pray, you must believe it, before you receive it. For we walk by faith, not by sight. (Romans 4:12)

You are to live by faith every day, believing and trusting in God to supply all your needs, for the just shall live by faith. (Romans 1:17)

"So then faith cometh by hearing and hearing the word of God" (Romans 10:17)

Your faith shall grow by hearing and hearing God's Word. You must speak what you believe and act on what you believe. Your faith will grow more rapidly when your ears hear your own mouth constantly speaking God's Word. Whatever you need in life your words must express your faith, you must hold fast to your confession of God's Word, because God will do exactly what His Words says he will do.

Jesus said have faith in God

"For verily I say unto you, that whosoever shall say unto this mountain, Be thou removed, and be thou cast into the sea; and shall not doubt in his heart, but shall believe that those things which he saith shall come to pass; he shall have whosoever he saith." (Mark 11:23)

Jesus said you can have what you say if you don't doubt the words that you speak, if you believe what you are saying Jesus said it will come to pass. Jesus said you can speak to the mountain and it shall obey you.

Your mountain could be a mountain of:

- Debt
- Sickness
- Fear
- Sin

Whatever your mountain is, speak to it, and it shall obey.

Mustard seed faith

"And the Lord said, If ye had faith as a grain of mustard seed, ye might say unto this sycamine tree, Be thou plucked up by the root, and be thou planted in the sea and it should obey you." (Luke 17:6)

Jesus said if you have faith as a grain of a mustard seed you can speak to a tree and it shall obey you.

Do you know what is made out of trees?

- Paper
- Money
- Mortgages

If you need **money**, speak to it. If you need **a house**, speak to it. If you want your **mortgage** paid off, speak to it. Jesus said the tree would obey your faith filled words. Jesus has given us the right to use his **name**, his **word**, his **power** and **authority**. The same Holy Spirit that created the Earth dwells in you. It doesn't take great faith to get things accomplished. The problem is that we don't use our faith like we supposed to.

"Faith worketh by love" (Galatians 5:6)

Do you know why your faith isn't working? If you have unforgiveness in your heart then your faith will not work for you. You must love everybody, even your enemies. If you aren't walking in love then you're not walking in faith.

God is waiting on you

God has done everything he's going to do for you. God is waiting on you to speak his Word. God watches over His Word to confirm it in our lives. God confirms His word with signs following.

Do you want to please God?

Before Enoch was translated, he had this testimony that he pleased God. (Hebrew 11:5)

Jesus said, "I always do those things that pleases the father." (John 8:29)

But without faith it is impossible to please him. For he that cometh to God must believe that he is, and that he is a rewarder of them that diligently seek him.

If you aren't using your faith, you aren't pleasing God. In order to please God you must use your faith.

Ask in faith

If you aren't receiving an answer, you need to speak out the promises of God. Too many Christians waver after awhile and allow their doubts to come out of their mouths. This negative confession cancels the results that would have been forth coming. "But let him ask in faith, nothing wavering. For he that wavereth is like a wave of the sea driven with the wind and tossed. (Wavering indicated unbelief, wavering shows that we really don't expect to receive from God.) For let not that man think that he shall receive any thing of the Lord. A double minded man is unstable in all his ways." (James 1:6-8)

Seven

Patience

<u>Do you know why most Christians aren't receiving from God?</u>

THE LACK OF patience has robbed most of us at one time or another. We want answers to our prayers and we want them now. Sometimes God answers immediately, sometimes he makes us wait. If we don't receive the answer immediately, we give up. The lack of patience has blocked more Christians from receiving from God than many of us realize. Sowing and reaping always take time. We can't rush this process. "To everything there is a season, and a time for every purpose under heaven." (Ecclesiastes 3:1)

<u>You reap what you sow</u>

"And let us not be weary in well doing: for in due season we shall reap, if we faint not." (Galatians 6:9)

God said we will reap if we **<u>don't give up</u>**. Our reaping depends on whether or not we get tired of waiting and give up. If we are to prosper, we must be patient. God doesn't lie, all of God promises are real, and we will reap—if we are patient.

<u>Sowing and reaping always takes time</u>

Many of us are expecting a return when our seeds haven't had time to take root and grow and produce a harvest. If you don't get a prompt answer, don't get discouraged, don't doubt God's Word, don't waver (wavering indicates unbelief). Don't allow doubt to come out of your mouth. In the

Christian life, there are trials and temptation successfully overcoming these adversities produces maturity and strong character. Don't resent troubles, when they come, pray for wisdom. God will supply all that you will need to face persecution or adversity. He will give you patience and keep you strong in times of trial.

Faith and patience works together

"That ye not be slothful, but followers of them who through faith and patience inherit the promises." (Hebrews 6:12)

Slothful—means—lazy

You won't receive a bountiful return if you are lazy, you must exercise both faith and patience to receive from God. You must follow the example of those who receive all that God had promised them because of their strong faith and patience. **Don't be lazy**, you must constantly read and study God's Word in order to find out exactly what your rights and privileges are and how to attain them. You must "study to show thyself approved unto God, a workman that needeth not to be ashamed, rightly divided the word of truth." (II Timothy 2:15). There isn't an easy way: bible study is hard work. If you want to prosper, you must be willing to pay the price of working hard at studying God's Word. You must not throw away your confidence in God because of lack of patience. "For ye have need of patience, that, after ye have done the will of God, ye might receive the promise." (Hebrew 10:36)

Wait on the Lord

"Wait on the Lord: be of good courage, and he shall strengthen thine heart: wait, I say, on the Lord." (Psalm 27:14)

Waiting on God is not easy. Often it seems that he isn't answering our prayers or doesn't understand the urgency of our situation. That kind of thinking implies that God is not in control or is not fair, But God is worth waiting for. Sometimes you have to wait, because often God uses waiting to refresh, renew, and teach us. Make good use of your waiting time by discovering what God may be trying to teach you.

Eight

Be A Giver

"... It is more blessed to give than to receive." (Acts 20:35)

GOD SAID THIS because, if you don't give anything, you won't receive anything. Giving starts the process of receiving from God. Every scripture that God says to give, is backed with a promise to receive.

When we give we are putting God first in our lives, this shows God that we trust him. The more we give to God, God will open more channels for us to receive from Him. Giving is a seed and if we sow it properly, God will see that we will receive a harvest. God doesn't need more money, God is showing us how to receive the blessing he has in store for us.

God gave his best gift

God gave us his son Jesus. Jesus came that we might have life and have it more abundantly. (John10:10)

"Every good gift and every perfect gift is from above, and cometh down from the Father of lights, with whom is no variableness, neither shadow of turning." (James 1:17)

"He that spared not his own Son, but delivered him up for us all, how shall he not with him also freely give us all things?" (Roman 8:32)

God gave his only son, why would He hold back anything else from us. Every gift that God gives us is good and perfect for any situation. God gives us material things like good health, food, home, and cars. God also gives us spiritual things like wisdom, faith, grace, peace, and eternal life. "According to his divine power hath given unto us all things that pertain unto life and godliness." (II Peter 1:3)

Will a man rob God?

Yet ye have robbed me, but ye say, wherein have we robbed thee? In tithes and offering.

Rob—means—to take something belonging to someone else.
Robber—means—one who steals.
Tithe—means—the tenth of one's income; to pay a tenth of one's income

Will a man rob God? **Yes**. If you haven't been giving your tithes to God, then you are a robber. You are taking something that belongs to someone else. God said, "You have robbed me in tithes and offering." You are stealing the ten percent which belongs to God. If you are stealing the tithe which is ten percent of your income, I know you are stealing the offering also. If you steal from God, I know you would steal from me too. We have some thieves in the church, stealing God's money. I rather steal from you, before I steal from God. The bible says, "The thief cometh not, but for to steal . . ." (John 10:10). You're stealing from God and the devil is stealing from you, as long as you continue to steal from God, the devil will continue to steal from you. The only way to stop the devil from stealing from you, you have to start giving, God said when you give your tithes he would stop the devil from stealing from you.

Hard times

If you don't give your tithes and offering ye are cursed, with a curse: For ye have robbed me: even this whole nation. The curse is found in Deuteronomy 28:15-68.

If you haven't been giving, you are going to have hard times, it isn't going to get any better: you are going to have problems you are going to struggle through life, because you don't have anyone to turn to. You need to stop making excuses, saying you can't afford to tithe, tithing is in the Old Testament. Or When the Lord blesses me, then I will tithe. "As a man thinketh in his heart so is he." (Proverb 23:7). If you keep thinking that way, you are never going to have enough. If you want to prosper you must line up your thinking with the Word of God.

<u>The blessing of the tithe</u>

"Bring ye all the tithes unto the storehouse (**church**), that there may be meat in mine house, and prove (**test**) me now herewith, saith the Lord of hosts, if I will not open you the windows of heaven and pour you out a blessing, that there shall not be room enough to receive it." (Malachi 3:10)

God said bring all your tithes, which is ten percent, not one percent, not five percent, but ten percent.

God said to test him. He said, "Test me now." Why wait, put God to the test by giving your tithes. God promised that he'll pour you out a blessing that you won't have room enough to receive it.

<u>"No weapon that is formed against me shall prosper;"</u> <u>(Isaiah 54:17)</u>

God said he would rebuke the devourer (**devil**) for your sakes. In this verse of scripture, God is speaking to farmers, but this same principle applies to us today. Whatever method the devil uses to try to steal these blessings, God himself will rebuke him. This verse of scripture is the only place in the bible where God says that he will rebuke the devil. When it comes to receiving the blessing from our tithes and offering. God makes certain that the devil doesn't steal your blessing.

Remember this

I believe the ten percent **tithes** should go to your local church and your offering on top of these tithes should go where the Lord leads you to give.

New Testament teaching on giving

Jesus said "Give and it shall be given unto you; good measure, pressed down, and shaken together, and running over, shall men give into your bosom." (Luke 6:38). When we give according to God's word, our gift will come back to us overflowing and running over. As you give generously to others, God will inspire other men and women to give back to you in good measures. There are many ways that God can bless you. If you need a job, a pay raise, a promotion, a home, a car, food for your children, or whatever your need may be, God will inspire others to give to you.

Nine

Ask

I BELIEVE THAT IF you follow these guidelines in this book, you can go to God and ask him anything and he will give it to you

"All things whatsoever ye shall ask in prayer, believing, ye shall receive." (Matthew 21:22)

Prayer—is talking to God

Jesus didn't say, you'll receive some of the things you ask for, He said **ALL** things you ask for in prayer, believing you shall receive. God doesn't want you to ask, just to be asking. God wants you to expect to receive when you ask. "For all things are possible to him that believeth." (Mark 9:23)

"Delight thyself also in the lord: and He shall give thee the desires of thine heart." (Psalm 37:4)

Desire—means—to long for: request

Ask and it shall be given to you

"Ask and it shall be given to you; seek and ye shall find; knock and it shall be opened unto you: **For everyone that asketh receiveth** and he that seeketh findeth; and to him that knocketh it shall be opened." (Matthew 7:7). Even though our heavenly "Father Knoweth what things ye have need of, before ye ask him." (Matthew 6:8). He still wants you to ask him.

How can God help you if you don't ever ask him for anything. Jesus said that everyone that asketh receiveth. Whatever you need from the Lord you must ask in faith (James 1:6). "And whatsoever we ask, we receive of him, because we keep (**obey**) his commandments, and do those things that are pleasing in his sight." (I John 3:22)

Good things for those who ask

"If ye then, being evil, know how to give good gifts unto your children, how much more shall your Father which is in heaven give good things to them that **ask him**? (Matthew 7:11). Jesus said, even evil men know how to give good gifts to their children. How **much more** shall your Father, which is in heaven give **good things** to them that ask. God loves you, He cares about you, and He wants to help you. "Now unto him that is able to do exceeding abundantly above all that we **ask** or **think**, according to the power that worketh in us." (Ephesians 3:20). God doesn't want his children to be sick. He wants his children to be in good health. He doesn't want his children to live in poverty or in lack. God wants his children to be prosperous. (III John 1:2). God wants you to have the best things in life, new car, new house, clothes, food on the table, anything that you need . . . . **Just ask him!**

Have confidence when you pray.

And this is the confidence that we have in him, that, if we **ask anything** according to his will (**Word**) He heareth us: and if **we know** that he heareth us. **Whatsoever we ask**, we know that **we have** petitions that we desired of him.

Let's look at these two verses of scriptures. They say the same things.

- We ask
- He hears us
- We know
- We have

Do you know what the will of God is for your life?
His will is his word.

Before Jesus left this earth, he told his disciples, I go to be with my father. My father will give whatever you ask **in my name**, until now you have not asked for anything: ask and you will receive, so that your happiness may be complete. (John 16:24)(**GNB**) There is power in the name of Jesus, there is healing in his name, there is peace in his name, there is joy in his name, there is deliverance in his name, whatever you need.

Find scriptures that pertain to what you need. Take these scriptures and make a prayer out of these words and pray it to the Father in the name of Jesus, and the Father will give you the answer you desire from him.

You have not, because you ask not

"Ye lust, and have not: ye kill and desire to have, and cannot obtain: ye fight and war, yet ye have not, because ye ask not. Ye ask, and receive not, because ye ask amiss, that ye may consume it upon your lust." (James 4: 2,3)

These people strongly desire things that they could not have. These people were constantly fussing and fighting and some were ready to kill over the things they wanted. I believe they would also steal it if they had a strong desire for it. The reason they didn't have what they wanted, because they didn't ask God for the things needed. And when they did ask they didn't receive because their motives were bad. They would ask for things to use for their own pleasures. If you follow these guidelines, God will give you the desires of your heart. (Psalm 37:4). Jesus said **ask** and it shall be given unto you. You don't have to fuss and fight, you don't have to steal and kill for the things you desire, because God is a rewarder to those who diligently seek him. (Hebrews 11:6). The Word of God says every good and perfect gift comes from God. (James 1:17). God created this Earth for his children. God wants you to have the best things in this life. As you follow these guidelines, the blessings of the Lord shall come upon you and overtake you. God bless you, so that you can be a blessing to someone else, not for your own pleasures.

Ten

Thanksgiving and Praise

(*Pray once, don't beg. God heard you the first time)

"In everything give thanks for this is the will of God in Christ Jesus concerning you"

PAUL WAS NOT teaching that we should thank God for everything that happens to us, but in everything. Evil does not come from God, so we should not thank him for evil, but when evil strikes, we can still be thankful for whom God is and for the good he can bring through the distress. You are not to give thanks to God for the adverse circumstances, for the sicknesses, or for the calamity, test or trial Satan sends your way, but in the midst of every trial or test we go through in life, we are to thank him for his goodness.

Praise God for his goodness

"Oh that men would praise the Lord for his goodness, and for his wonderful works to the children of men! And let them sacrifice the sacrifices of thanksgiving, and declare his works with rejoicing." (Psalm 107:21, 22)

You are to praise God for his goodness, for good health, eternal life, strength, food, clothes, shelter, for everything. You can praise God anywhere or anytime, you can praise God while driving down the road, and you can praise God while walking down the street. Your praises to God don't have to be loud to be effective, you can praise the Lord quietly to yourself so no one is disturbed or you can get somewhere by yourself and praise God wholeheartedly with a loud voice. When you don't feel like praising God, praise him anyway. That's what you call the **sacrifice of praise**.

Thank—means—to express gratitude
Thankfulness—means—gratefulness to another
Praise—means—extolling God for what he has done and is doing for you
Worship—means—extolling God simply for who he is

The power of praise

Whatever you are facing in your life. If you will learn how to praise God before you see the answer, God will give you the victory. Whatever you need from God, it's available right now if you'll begin to take God at his Word and praise him for the provisions he has already made for you in his Word. You can get anything you need from God if you'll learn to constantly praise God and obey his Word. The power of God is real. The power of God is available to set you free, you can tap into that power by praise. You bring the demonstration of God's power into your circumstance by praising Him. The power of God will come on the scene to set you free.

God inhabits your praises

Inhibits—means—to dwell, occupy, reside or stay

Praise brings you directly into contact with God, because the bible says God inhabits the praises of his people. (Psalm 22:3)

If you want to bring the presence and the power of God into your midst to change any circumstance or any situation you're facing in your life, begin to praise God continuously from the heart. His power will change that situation. God will work it out for you, because God inhabits your praises, and where God is, there is victory. "O, give thanks unto the Lord; for he is good: because his mercy endureth forever." (Psalm 118:1) You can never thank God enough because he is good and his mercy endures forever.

Praise brings victory

"I will bless the Lord at all times: his praise shall continually be in my mouth." (Psalm 34:1)

Jesus defeated the devil. The victory has already been won for you in every circumstance, every trial, and in every test you will ever face in life. Now it's up to you by the praises of your mouth to cause the victory Jesus already won for you on Calvary to manifest in every area of your life. Be determined to praise the Lord at all times and in all situations. The praises of your mouth will bring you the success you've been waiting for. Your praise and your obedience to God's Word will determine whether you attain your goals in life.

Praise bring increase

"Let the people praise thee, O God; let all the people praise thee. Then shall the earth yield her increases; and God even our own God, shall bless us." (Psalm 67: 5,6)

Increase comes as a result of praise. Praise recognizes and gives God the credit even before the answer is manifested. If you need an increase in your life, begin to praise God that's what this verse is saying: then shall the earth yield her increase (Psalm 67:6). Sincere praise moves God and put him first in your life, God will make those things which concern you, prosper for you. If you need an increase in your life or any kind, spiritually, physically, or materially, set aside some time to seek God and put his Word first. Then praise God, who hears and answers prayers. Praise receives the answers by faith, and praise is giving thanks to God before the answer is seen. There is a proper time to exercise prayer and a proper time to praise. Both prayer and praise are necessary and important, but after you've prayed and believed God for the answer based on the word, that's the time to stay in faith by praising him. **"Give thanks always for all things unto God the Father in the name of our Lord Jesus Christ." (Ephesians 5:20)**

BOOK ORDER FORM

To order additional books by Larry Ellerbee, directly from the publisher, please use this order form. You can also visit our website
www.learnhowtoreceivefromgod.com

Book Title	Price	Qty	Amount
10 Guidelines on How to Receive from God	$15.99 paperback _____		$ _____
	$24.99 hardback _____		$ _____

Total Book Amount ....$ _____
Shipping and Handling
Add $4.50 + $ 1.10 for each book..$ _____

Total order amount enclosed ....$ _____

Check or Money Order
Make check or money order payable to: Larry Ellerbe

Mail Order to: Larry Ellerbe
             8613 Amish Drive
             Fayetteville, NC 28314

Please print your name, address, and phone number clearly:

Name: _____

Street Address: _____

City: _____

State or Province: _____

Zip or Postal Code: _____

Telephone Number: (_____) _____-_____

<u>Foreign orders must be submitted in U.S. dollars</u>. Foreign orders are shipped by uninsured surface mail. We ship all orders within 48 hours of receipt of order.

10 Guidelines on How to Receive From God

The Bible is God's Instruction Book; we are to follow His instructions in order to receive from him.

Psalm 25: 4—Shew me thy ways, O Lord: Teach me thy paths.
Isaiah 55: 8, 9—God said my ways are higher than your ways.

This book was written with the purpose of teaching you God's way to health, wealth, happiness, security, and peace of mind. *The 10 Guidelines on How to Receive From God* will teach you how to reach the source of your good, and get the desired results that you have been seeking.

Follow these easy and simple Guidelines and God will bring success into your life.

As you follow these Guidelines outlined in this book, you'll discover the power of God, that can lift you out of a state of frustration, illness, loneliness, discord, and poverty; God can set you up on the high road to happiness health, and freedom.

Jesus said, If thou canst believe, all things are possible to him(her) that believeth (Mark 9:23)

Printed in Great Britain
by Amazon.co.uk, Ltd.,
Marston Gate.